First World War
and Army of Occupation
War Diary
France, Belgium and Germany

57 DIVISION
Divisional Troops
Loyal North Lancashire Regiment
2/5th Battalion (Territorial Force)
1 June 1917 - 31 May 1919

WO95/2974/3

The Naval & Military Press Ltd
www.nmarchive.com
Published in association with The National Archives

Published by

The Naval & Military Press Ltd

Unit 10 Ridgewood Industrial Park,

Uckfield, East Sussex,

TN22 5QE England

Tel: +44 (0) 1825 749494

www.naval-military-press.com

www.nmarchive.com

This diary has been reprinted in facsimile from the original. Any imperfections are inevitably reproduced and the quality may fall short of modern type and cartographic standards.

© Crown Copyright
Images reproduced by permission of The National Archives, London, England, 2015.

Contents

Document type	Place/Title	Date From	Date To
Heading	WO95/2974-3		
Heading	2-5th Loyal Nth Lancs (Pioneers) Feb 1918-May 1919 57 Div From 170 Bde		
Heading	War Diary Of 2/5 Loyal North Lancashire Regt. (Pioneers) From Feb 1st 1918 To Feb 28th 1918		
War Diary	Wezmacquart Section	01/02/1918	05/02/1918
War Diary	Erquinghem	05/02/1918	14/02/1918
War Diary	Estaires Area	15/02/1918	28/02/1918
Heading	War Diary Of 2/5 Bn. Loyal N. Lancs Regt. (P) From March 1st 1918-March 31st 1918		
War Diary	Estaires Area	01/03/1918	19/03/1918
War Diary	Sailly	20/03/1918	31/03/1918
Heading	2/5th Battalion The Loyal North Lancashire Regt Pioneers April 1918		
Heading	War Diary Of 2/5. Bn. Loyal North. Lancs. Regt. (Pioneers) From April 1st 1917 To April 30th 1917.		
War Diary	Sailly Sur La Lys	01/04/1918	01/04/1918
War Diary	Caudecure	02/04/1918	04/04/1918
War Diary	Pommera	05/04/1918	08/04/1918
War Diary	Marieux	09/04/1918	12/04/1918
War Diary	Humbercourt	13/04/1918	13/04/1918
War Diary	Authie	14/04/1918	16/04/1918
War Diary	Coigneux	17/04/1918	06/05/1918
War Diary	H.Q. At Coigneux	07/05/1918	27/05/1918
War Diary	Coigneux	28/05/1918	31/05/1918
Miscellaneous	Report On Defence Works-Week-Ending 15/16 5.18		
Miscellaneous	Report On Defence Works For Week Ending 23.5.18		
Miscellaneous	Weekly Report On Defence Works For Week Ending 29/30/5/18		
War Diary	Coigneux	01/06/1917	30/06/1917
Miscellaneous	2/5 Bn. Loyal North Lancs Rgt. (P) Summary Of Work Completed During The Period May 7th/8th. To June 12th. 1918.	13/06/1918	13/06/1918
Miscellaneous	2/5 Bn. Loyal North Lancs Rgt. (P) Supplementary Summary Of Work Completed During The Period Of June 12th. To June 29th. 1918.	29/06/1918	29/06/1918
Miscellaneous	Work Completed During The Period May 7th/8th. To June 29th/-1918	29/06/1918	29/06/1918
Miscellaneous	Weekly Report On Defence Works For Week Ending 6/6/18		
Miscellaneous	Weekly Report On Defence Works For Week Ending 13.6.18 Ref. Sheet 57p1/20000		
Miscellaneous	Weekly Report On Defence Works For Week Ending 20.6.18 Ref Sheet 57/D.N.E/20,000		
Miscellaneous	2/5th Loyal N Lancs. Regt. (P). Weekly Report On Defence Works For Week Ending 27.6.18 (6.0 A.M.)		
War Diary	Coigneux	01/07/1918	02/07/1918
War Diary	St Leger-Les-Authie	03/07/1918	29/07/1918
War Diary	Grouches	30/07/1918	31/07/1918

Heading	War Diary Of 2/5 Bn. Loyal North Lancs. From August 1st 1918 To Aug 31st 1918		
War Diary	Wanquetin	01/08/1918	01/08/1918
War Diary	Arras	02/08/1918	18/08/1918
War Diary	Marquay	19/08/1918	22/08/1918
War Diary	Noyelles-Vion	22/08/1918	22/08/1918
War Diary	Beaudricourt	25/08/1918	25/08/1918
War Diary	Bavincourt	26/08/1918	27/08/1918
War Diary	Blaireville	27/08/1918	30/08/1918
War Diary	Sheet 51 B 1/40,000 N.35.a.9.6.	30/08/1918	31/08/1918
Heading	War Diary Of 2/5 Bn. Loyal North Lancs. From Sept 1st 1918 To Sept 30th 1918		
War Diary	Sheet 51 b 1/40,000 N.35.a.9.6	01/09/1918	03/09/1918
War Diary	O15c.8.6	04/09/1918	07/09/1918
War Diary	U15c.8.6.	07/09/1918	07/09/1918
War Diary	Queant	07/09/1918	16/09/1918
War Diary	St Leger	17/09/1918	29/09/1918
War Diary	E.22.c.2.6.	30/09/1918	30/09/1918
Heading	War Diary Of 2/5 Loyal North Lancs. From October 1st 1918 To Oct 31.1918		
War Diary	57.c.NE. E.22.c.2.6.	01/10/1918	01/10/1918
War Diary	Fontaine Notre Dame	02/10/1918	10/10/1918
War Diary	Moeuvres	11/10/1918	12/10/1918
War Diary	Noeux-Les-Mines	13/10/1918	14/10/1918
War Diary	Fromelles	15/10/1918	16/10/1918
War Diary	Radinghem	17/10/1918	18/10/1918
War Diary	Canteleu	19/10/1918	20/10/1918
War Diary	Lezennes	21/10/1918	27/10/1918
War Diary	Cornet	28/10/1918	31/10/1918
Heading	War Diary November 2/5 L.N. Lancs Vol 22		
War Diary	Ronchin	01/11/1918	10/11/1918
War Diary	Ronchin	10/11/1918	10/11/1918
War Diary	Blandain	11/11/1918	11/11/1918
War Diary	Tournai	12/11/1918	30/11/1918
War Diary		01/11/1918	30/11/1918
Heading	War Diary 2/5 L.N. L.R. (P) Vol 23		
War Diary	Ronchin	01/12/1918	02/12/1918
War Diary	Camphin	03/12/1918	03/12/1918
War Diary	Arras	04/12/1918	31/12/1918
Heading	2/5 Bn. Loyal North Lancs Regt War Diary January 1919 Vol 24		
War Diary	Arras	01/01/1919	31/01/1919
Heading	War Diary Feb 1919 2/5 L.N. L.R. Vol 25		
War Diary	Arras	01/02/1919	28/02/1919
War Diary	Arras	31/03/1919	31/03/1919
Heading	War Diary March 1919 2/5 Loyal North Lancs Regt Vol 26		
War Diary	Maroeuil	13/03/1919	31/03/1919
War Diary	Arras	01/03/1919	18/03/1919
War Diary	Maroeuil	19/03/1919	31/03/1919
War Diary	Maroeuil	08/03/1919	28/03/1919
Heading	War Diary 2/5 Loyal North Lancs April 1919 Vol 27		
War Diary	Maroeuil	01/04/1919	30/04/1919
Heading	War Diary Of 2/5 Bn Loyal North Lancs Regt May 1919 Vol 28		
War Diary	Maroeuil	01/05/1919	31/05/1919

WD 9 cm / 2974 (3)

WD 7 cm / 2019 Rupee (3)

57TH DIVISION

2-5TH LOYAL NTH LANCS (PIONEERS)
FEB 1918 - MAY 1919

57 DIV FROM 170 Bde

13.

WM 13

— CONFIDENTIAL —

WAR DIARY

OF

2/5 LOYAL NORTH LANCASHIRE REGT. (PIONEERS)

FROM FEB 1ST 1918
TO FEB. 28TH 1918.

WAR DIARY
or
INTELLIGENCE SUMMARY.
(Erase heading not required.)

Army Form C. 2118.

FEBRUARY 1918.

13.

Place	Date	Hour	Summary of Events and Information	Remarks and references to Appendices
WEZMACQUART			Strength of Battalion 41 officers 640 Orants.	
SECTION	1/2/18	12.0 noon		
	1/2/18	7.0 p.m.	The Battalion relieved the 1/5 Bn. King's Own R. Regt. in close support with 1 Coy. garrisoning PLOEGRIE SWITCH and 3 Coys in Old Serbia Line.	
	5/2/18	5.30 pm	The Battalion was relieved by the 7th Bn. L.N. Lanc. Regt. and took over billets in ERQUINGHEM.	
ERQUINGHEM	5/2/18	6 pm	Owing to the re-organization of Brigade on a 3 Battalion basis the Battalion was selected to be the "PIONEER BATTALION" to the Division on From. 6 pm. 5/2/18.	
- do -	5/2/18 6 p.m.		The Battalion worked on the improvement of our defences of the Divisional Section under orders of C.R.E. 57th Divn.	
- do -	10/2/18		The following drafts arrived } 9 Officers + 230 rank from 8th Bn. L.N. Lanc.	
- do -	11/2/18		and were taken on Strength } 150 Oants from 7th Bn. L.N. Lanc.	
- do -	14/2/18	9.4 am	The Battalion moved to ESTAIRES AREA and relieved and took over the units in hand of the 1/5 Bn. Welsh Regt. (Pioneers)	
			Coys. billeted as follows. A Coy. at. G.32.b.50.95. C Coy. at G.34.d.5.4.	
			B. Coy. at G.34.a.7.9. D Coy. at 1. 26.a.3.6.	
			HQ G 32.a.9.9.	

Army Form C. 2118.
13.

WAR DIARY
or
INTELLIGENCE SUMMARY.
(Erase heading not required.)

FEBRUARY 1918

Place	Date	Hour	Summary of Events and Information	Remarks and references to Appendices
ESTAIRES AREA	16/2/18 to 25/2/18		A & B Coys worked under the orders of C.R.E. 15 Corps. and C & D Coys worked under orders of C.R.E. 12th Division. All Companies worked on the improvement of the defences of the 12 & 15 Div Area.	
	28/2/18		The Battalion in accordance with orders received and G.H.Q. O.B. 2155 of 13/2/18 was reorganized on a 3 Company basis. The reduction to new establishment will be gradually effected by allowing natural attrition to take its course, and not by at once transferring surplus personnel. Strength of Battalion. 51 officers 968 O. Ranks	
	28/2/18			

CONFIDENTIAL.

WAR DIARY

OF

2/5 Bn. LOYAL N. LANCS. REGT (?)

From

March 1st 1918 — March 31st 1918.

Army Form C. 2118.

WAR DIARY
or
INTELLIGENCE SUMMARY.
(Erase heading not required.)

MARCH 1918

Place	Date	Hour	Summary of Events and Information	Remarks and references to Appendices
ESTAIRES AREA	1/3/18 - 9/3/18		Strength of Battalion:- 53 Officers 926. O.R. The Battalion carried on with Work as follows:- M.G. emplacements under C.R.E. 55th Corps. Working in Trench M.G. emplacements. Signal dug-outs. 1/2 companies working under C.R.E. 55th Division on Meuhaux defences.	
- do -	10/3/18	6 p.m.	C Company Billets shelled. Casualties Killed 16. O.R. Wounded 14 O.R.	
	11/3/18 - 14/3/18		Companies worked as above.	
	12/3/18	2 p.m.	The Battalion was inspected by the G.O.C. 57th Division.	
	15/3/18		Work as above.	
	19/3/18		Casualties in "B" Coy with 19th. Killed - 2 O.R. Wounded 1 Officer 7 O.R.	
	24/3/18		The battalion relieved the 5th Northamptonshire Regt (P) and took over billets as follows:-	
SAILLY	29/3/18		B.H.Q. Ghd.5.1. B Coy. G.27a.3.9. A Coy. H.19.e.0.8. C Coy. G.16.c.9.5.	

WAR DIARY
or
INTELLIGENCE SUMMARY.
(Erase heading not required.)

Army Form C. 2118.

Place	Date	Hour	Summary of Events and Information	Remarks and references to Appendices
SAILLY	21/3/18	—	The Battalion now commenced work under C.R.E. 51st Division as follows:—	
			A Coy. — Work on Yeuhuin Defences.	
			B " — Making C.T. from Windy Post to Eeles Avenue.	
			C " — Joining up [?] points with a Trench Tunnel from Chated Post to Mt. Central.	
			One platoon of A Coy was detached for work in Gunnerys under the Corps Drawing Office.	
			Gas casualties — 15	
-do-	21/3/18	10 a.m.	Work as taken on the 21st inst	
-do-	22/3/18	—	— do —	
-do-	25/3/18	—	— do —	
-do-	26/3/18	—		
-do-	27/3/18	—	Companies commenced working as follows:—	
-do-	28/3/18	—	A — Working under 502 Fd. Coy. (less 2 secs. under M.G.H. on M.G. shelters)	
			B " " " 424 " " " " " " " " " "	
			C " " " 505 " " " " " " " " " "	

WAR DIARY
or
INTELLIGENCE SUMMARY.

(Erase heading not required.)

Place	Date	Hour	Summary of Events and Information	Remarks and references to Appendices
SAILLY	29/3/18	—	Work as for the 28th inst. Casualties: 1 O.R. Killed, 1 O.R. Wounded (slightly).	
—do—	30/3/18	—	Work as on the 29th inst.	
—do—	31/3/18	—	—do—	
			Strength of Battalion :— 53 Officers, 874 O.R.	

57th Divisional Pioneers

WAR DIARY

2/5th BATTALION

THE LOYAL NORTH LANCASHIRE REGT

Pioneers

APRIL 1918

CONFIDENTIAL.

Vol 15

WAR DIARY.

OF.

2/5. Bn. LOYAL NORTH. LANCS. REGT. (PIONEERS)

FROM. APRIL. 1st 1917.   TO. APRIL 30th 1917.

Army Form C. 2118.

WAR DIARY
or
INTELLIGENCE SUMMARY.
(Erase heading not required.)

APRIL

Place	Date	Hour	Summary of Events and Information	Remarks and references to Appendices
SAILLY SUR LA LYS.	1/4/18		Strength of battalion 53 Officers 870 O.R.	
-do-	1/4/18	11 a.m.	Moved by road to CAVOESCURE (MERVILLE AREA)	
CAVOESCURE	2/4/18		Billeted in CAVOESCURE	
	3/4/18		Marched to Station at CALONNE SUR LA LYS. Entrained for MONDICOURT. Detrained and marched to LA SOUICH to billets.	
	4/4/18		Marched to billets in POMMERA	
POMMERA	5/4/18			
	6/4/18		Training and interior economy.	
	7/4/18			
	8/4/18		Marched to MARIEUX AERODROME.	
-do-	9/4/18			
MARIEUX	9/4/18 - 11/4/18		Training.	
-do-	11/4/18		Marched to billets in HUMBERCOURT.	
HUMBERCOURT	13/4/18		" " Advance in AUTHIE WOOD.	
AUTHIE	14/4/18		Informing & constructing camp.	
-do-	15/4/18		Work on rear defences.	

15

WAR DIARY

INTELLIGENCE SUMMARY.

(Erase heading not required.)

Army Form C. 2118.

Instructions regarding War Diaries and Intelligence Summaries are contained in F. S. Regs., Part II. and the Staff Manual respectively. Title pages will be prepared in manuscript.

Place	Date	Hour	Summary of Events and Information	Remarks and references to Appendices
LA THIEU	4/4/18	8 a.m.	Marched to COIGNEUX. and bivouaced.	
COIGNEUX	19/4/18 - 30/4/18		Work on LA HAIE SWITCH (back area defence), in the vicinity of SAULTY AU BOIS, SOUASTRE and FONQUEVILLERS. Casualties during the month — Nil	
	30/4/8	noon	Strength of battalion 51 officers, 850 O.R.	

WAR DIARY
INTELLIGENCE SUMMARY.
(Erase heading not required)

2/5 LN Lumb Rgt
N68. Army Form C. 2118.
MAY 1918

Place	Date	Hour	Summary of Events and Information	Remarks and references to Appendices
Gomiecourt	1st	-	Strength of Battalion :- 51 Officers, 843 O.R. Work on the HAIE SWITCH (Back Area defences) in the vicinity of SALLY AU BOIS, SOUASTRE and FONQUEVILLERS	
	2nd-5th	-	- do -	
	6th	-	Relieved the 1/4 Northumberland Fusiliers in forward area. Distribution as follows :- HQrs :- COIGNEUX A & B :- GOMMECOURT PARK C :- SALLY AU BOIS	
H.Q. at COIGNEUX	7th	-	Work taken over was commenced as follows :- ① A & B Coys :- Digging a new C.T. across No Man's land, joining up the old British and German front lines in front of GOMMECOURT PARK. ② C Coy :- Constructing a new Brigade H.Q. at LA HAIE CHATEAU. Constructing M.G. dugouts in front of LA HAIE CHATEAU	

WAR DIARY
or
INTELLIGENCE SUMMARY.

Army Form C. 2118.

Place	Date	Hour	Summary of Events and Information	Remarks and references to Appendices
HQ at COIG/NEWS	8th 9th 10th 11th 12th 13th		Work as for the 7th inst. Casualties:- 2 officers Wounded (Capt S. Rathbone and Lieut. W. M. Munro — and gunners) Work as above. Also reconnoitering an old German trench in front of LA HAIE CHATEAU. (Wounded 2 O.R's).	14/5/15 and gunners
– do –	14th		– do –	
– do –	15th		– do –	
– do –	16th		– do –	
– do –	17th		– do –	
– do –	18th		– do –	
– do –	22nd		– do –	
– do –	23rd & 24th		Work as above.	
	25th		– do –	Casualties. Killed 3 O.R. Wounded 2 O.R.
	26th		– do –	Casualties. Killed 1 O.R.
	27th		– do –	Casualties. Wounded 1 O.R.

Army Form C. 2118.

WAR DIARY
or
INTELLIGENCE SUMMARY.
(Erase heading not required)

Place	Date	Hour	Summary of Events and Information	Remarks and references to Appendices
COIGNEUX	28th		Work as for the 24th inst	
	29th		—do—	
	30th		—do—	
	31st		—do— Casuals Wounded 1 O.R.	
			Strength of Battalion 39 Officers 876 O.R.	

REPORT ON DEFENCE WORKS — WEEK ENDING 15/5/18 (12 NOON).

NATURE OF WORK	LOCATION	No. OF NEW	COY.	BN.	FACTOR OF COMPLETION	REMARKS
Wire	Nil					
Trenches or Saps	E.P.C. 13.05		105	A	90%	New C.T. (Gunner's C.T.) approach over No Man's Land. 100 chunk knife rests.
Posts	K. 40. 5. 25					Gun pits made for 2 both Van L.G.
	K. 40. 35. 50			A		New trench joining up C.T. (approx. 200 yds)
	K. 40. 36. 25	6 o.p.			50%	New C.T. (Morgan C.T.) dug 12' (3' x 3') (to be 9' x 3') to complete. 70% Approx 100 yds of the C.T. excavated.
NEW C.T.	E. 28a. 28. 80. 10				35%	
	E. 28c. 60. 30		14	B		
	E. 29a. 20. 10. 16		145	B	65%	New C.T. (from 29a. 10. 16 to E. 29c. 55. 30) 35% completed. Dug to depth 3'4". Next Sump put in 2' x 2' x 3'4".
	E. 29c. 60. 56					
	E. 28a. 05. 90. 16		156	B	Complete	"STOUT TRENCH" (Preliminary ob. Bank raised to use as C.T.)
	E. 28a. 20. 70. 16		167	B	20%	Reclaiming old C.T.
C.T's TO BE RECLAIMED	E. 29a. 90. 75. 16		150	B	50%	Reclaimed one C.T. running over Kent.
	E. 20a. 30. 70. 16					
	E. 20a. 30. 40			C	Do	Work progress report from 5D2 Fitter Bay 16 Men left behind & 3 steps.
Dugout's (New)	K. 1. a. 2. 4.			C	Do	
Do	N.C.					
	R. 26. 2.2.				Do	A.C. Report
Dugouts (Extension)	(New trench to extended old)			B	Do	No. dugout crew fitted. Dugout's occupied for B. Boy. 8 Extra Do Do.
Ant as Mark.	Run. TRENCH E 28.90			C	Do	G. Coy Bullets
Cellar Gutter	Nil				Do	
N.C. Stations	Nil		A	Do		
General Road	Forward Area			B	Do	Roads this squad where hidden previously through crossing tracks on bridges.
(Junction)	E. 29a. 26. 10		8	A	Do	
	E. 19a. 66. 75		5		Completed	Repairing water men over poles. Pulling tramways.
(Tramways)	Forward Area					

SHEET N° 1.   REPORT ON DEFENCE WORKS FOR WEEK ENDING 23.5.18

REF. SHEET 57.D 1/20,000.

NATURE OF WORK	LOCATION	N° OF MEN	COY.	BATT'N	FACTOR OF COMPLETION	REMARKS
1. WIRE. (Giving nature of wire & thickness.)	Wiring southern sides of GUINNESS C.T. K:3.b.60.00 to K.4.a. 03.15.	1 Officer & 32. O.R's.	A	2/5 N.I.R.	90%	Hop'lands 3' high two fences 9' knee wire complete. Cross fences to form compartments to be made.
2. TRENCHES OR STRONG POINTS (Dug or under construction).	K:4.d.30.35 to K:10.a.55.90.	272.	A & B	Do.	90%	RUM TRENCH 50 yards junction of RUM TRENCH & NAMELESS TRENCH (not yet completed. Dug to first belt 44½'. 3 ft. S.P's in RUM TRENCH (K.4.d 2.3. (?)K.4.c. 7.0. Complete (dugouts to be made).
	K:10.a. 55.90 to K:10.a.15.98.	119.	A & B Station T.C.	Do.	50%	
	E.27.d. 76.05 to K.4.a.15.30.	105.	A.	Do.	Complete	GUINNESS C.T. 300 yds duckboards laid & wired on southern side, trench drained
	E.28.c. 30.5. to E.28.c.05.00.	147.	B.	Do.	40%	ALLSOPPS C.T. 110 yds to be completed to required width & depth. duckboards to be laid.
	K.3.b 80.10. To K.3.d 60.90.	32.	A.	Do.	Made & pilable.	
	K. 3.d 90.50.	27.	A.	Do.	45%	A. Coy's Batt'le Positions
	K. 4.a. 10.10.	26.	A.	Do.	90%	
	K. 3.b. 3.3.	25.	A.	Do.	Made & pilable.	
	K.1.b 1.1.To K.2.a. 1/0.50.	33.	A.	Do.	90%	As Reported by 502 Cov. Field R.E.
	K. 1.a. 2.4.	40.	C.	Do.		As Reported by 502 Field Coy R.E.
	K. 2.d. 2.2.	32.	C.	Do.		Lt Marrin 4th Tyneed. N.C.Dugout
3. DUGOUTS Completed or under construction.	Nil.					
4. DUGOUTS fitted with anti gas blankets.	Nil.					
5. M.G. Positions Constructed or under construction.	Nil.					

Weekly Report on Defence Works for week ending 29/30/5/18

Nature of work	Location	No. of Men	Coy. Batt.	% stage of Completion	Remarks
1. WIRE (Giving nature of wire & thickness)	Wiring RUN TR. (K95 90.90. To K.19a 35.90 and K4.d 36.H0'	40	A	whole length finished 30th June 1918	Booby's B.A Fence 4250yds Ba Fence behind eastern Cousins (total 4450yds D.9 Fence 50yds P.A fence 140yds (3 belts thick) 9 Linear bay thickness with loose wire
	Wiring GONNECOURT TR. K.5a.84.40 to K.5a.88.55	—	"	whole track completed 15/6	
2. TRENCHES OR STRONG POINTS (Dug or under construction)	RUN TRENCH. K.10a.10.99. K.10a.30.80. K.4.42. 20.20 to K.H.d. 30.35	32	B.	70%	Lench widened & deepened to take Lotters near Dump for dug completed at K4.d. 00.20 (H Small Elephant) Shelter 50% complete at K. HC. 90 90.
	GUINNESS C.T. E.24.d. 75. 06. To K.4a. 15.30	65	A	Complete	Duckboarding complete
	ALLSOPP C.T. E.28c.20.45. to E.23.d. 05.90	12	A	95%	Rucys 30% complete at E28c 90.80. Newtrench completed at E.27c.30.75. 25yds Duckboard laid
	GONNECOURT TR. E.29.c. 60.95. E.29.b.8.1.70. E.29.b.90.15.	24	B	50%	Doyle Trench widened & deepened (New section posts at K5a.60.55. 9x 6a.43.75. 2 Small Elephant shelter at E.29.c.65. 6.6 y E.29.c.70.70 (H59 complete) New section posts complete K5a.60.55
	K.1b.11. To K.2a.40.60.	52 33	B HQ		Act Opened by 502 Field Coy R.E col & Lunch Refreshments
3. DUGOUTS Completed or under construction	K.1a. 2.4. K.20.2.2.1.	40 32	C C		Ac Reported by 502 Field Coy R.E 30 Newing Sets Issued (M.G dugout) Point Batts 4450yds
	Jap 35.98	5	HQ	95%	
4. Dugouts (Keep nyt sent by Geo Blanket)	GONNECOURT PARK KEEPS	31	C.		2 dugout & Entrance complete (entrance frames)
5. M G Position completed or under constn.	Nil				
6. General (Roads Tramways)	Forward Area. Do Do J. 3.D	4 6 2	A A HQ		Oxford Avenue & Well hole tilted in whole as necessary Tramways repaired where broken & where necessary Assisting 502 Field Coy R.E in Subterranean Passage excavation

2/5 LN Rams Regt P
Army Form C. 2118.
June 1917

WAR DIARY
or
INTELLIGENCE SUMMARY.

Place	Date	Hour	Summary of Events and Information	Remarks and references to Appendices
COIGNEU	1st		Strength of Battalion :– 39 officers 833 O.R. Work in forward defences in GOMMECOURT PARK. Distribution :– (a) A, & B Coys; 2 platoons of C Coy in GOMMECOURT PARK. (b) 2 platoons of C Coy. at RAYEN COURT. (c) Headquarters at COIGNEUX. Casualties :– Wounded – 3 O.R.	
	2nd		Work as above. Wounded – 2 O.R's	
	3rd		— do —	
	4th–8th		Work as above.	
	9th–16th		New C.T. dug east of GOMME COURT. Work as for 16th inst.	
	17th			
	19th			
	20th		Work commenced in BRER TRENCH. Construction	99
	21st		of 50 baby elephant shelters	
	–30th			

WAR DIARY
or
INTELLIGENCE SUMMARY

Army Form C. 2118.

JUNE

Place	Date	Hour	Summary of Events and Information	Remarks and references to Appendices
Cuinchy			Casualties from 4 - 30/6/16	
			7th. Wounded 1 O.R.	
			9th. Killed 1 O.R.	
			14th. Wounded 1 O.R. Wounded 3 O.R.	
			15th. " (Since died of Wounds).	
			25 " 2 O.R.	
			1 O.R.	
			Took over in the 29th inst.	
Cuinchy 30th			Strength of Battalion - 39 Officers. 758. O.R.	

2/5 BN. LOYAL NORTH LANCS RGT.(P)
SUMMARY OF WORK COMPLETED DURING THE PERIOD
MAY 7th/8th. TO JUNE 12th. 1918.

1. **WIRING**

   (a) **GUINNESS C.T.**

   Erected 460 yds. Triple (High) Fence with Standard pattern knee wire from E.27.d.65.05. to K.4.a.10.25.

   (b) **RUM TRENCH.**

   Erected 200 yds. double apron fence from K.9.b.90.95. to K.10.a.35.90., 50 yds. double apron fence at K.4.d.35.40., 450 yds. double apron fence from K.9.b.90.99. to K.10.a.35.70, and 200 yds. double apron fence from K.9.b.90.90. to K.10.a.30.70.

   (c) **GOMMECOURT TRENCH.**

   Erected 400 yds. Triple fence from K.5.a.70.40. to K.5.a.75.80., inner bays thickened with loose wire, and 350 yds. double apron fence from E.30.a.15.15. to E.29.d.50.85.

2. **TRENCHES.**

   (a) **GUINNESS C.T.(New Trench)**

   Excavated 460 yds. of trench to Corps Pattern from E.27.d.75.05. to K.4.a.20.35. with Fire steps made facing both flanks. Trench drained and duckboarded, sump pit excavated.

   (b) **GUINNES C.T.(Old Portion)**

   Excavated 220 yds. of new trench to connect old C.Ts. from K.4.c.85.55. to K.4.d.25.45.

FORWARD

"(Con*d.)

(c) ALLSOPPS C.T. (New Trench)

    Excavated 480 yds. of trench to Corps Pattern from E.28.c.25.80. to E.28.d.05.85. Drained and duckboarded. 2 Sump pits excavated.

(d) ALLSOPPS C.T. (Old Portion).

    Widened, deepened, and cleared 450 yds. of trench from E.28.d.05.85. to E.28.b.70.45.

    Cleared, drained, and revetted 300 yds. from E.29.a.20.10. to E.28.b.70.45.

(e) BENTS AVENUE. (New Trench)

    Excavated 400 yds. of new trench from E.29.a.20.10. to E.29.c.45.80. Trench drained, and sump pit excavated.

(f) TRAM TRENCH

    Cleaned out 250 yds. of trench from E.30.c.45.10. to E.29.d.90.15.

(g) RUM TRENCH

    Widened, deepened, and reconstructed to Corps Pattern, 850 yds. from K.4.d.30.35. to K.9.b.90.99. Section Posts constructed at K.4.d.20.30. and K.4.c.70.00.

(h) COMMECOURT TRENCH.

    Widened and deepened 300 yds. from E.29.b.90.10. to E.29.d.50.90., and at E.29.c.69.65. Section Posts completed at K.5.a. 70.70. and E.29.c.65.65.

(i) OLD FRENCH TRENCH.

    Cleared and repaired 350 yds. of trench from K.1.b.1.1. to K.20.a.70.50. Fire bays reconstructed. (Work under 502 Field Coy.R.E.)

Forward.

(Con'd.)   3.

        (j) BATTLE POSITIONS.

           Constructed Platoon Battle positions at K.3.b.80.10., K.3.d.90.50., K.4.a.10.10., and K.3.b.30.30.

3. DUGOUTS.

    (a) M.G. H.Q. dugout at K.2.d.2.2. 75% complete.

    (b) Excavated Brigade H.Q. at K.1.a.2.4. (work under 502 Field Coy.R.E.)

    (c) Constructed 6 small Elephant Shelters in Post at K.4.c.90.00., 4 at E.29.c.65.65. and E.29.c.70.70., 2 at E.29.c.90.85., 2, 28% completed at K.3.d.99.05., 2, 10% completed, at K.4.c.05.10. 3, 50% completed, at E.29.d.25.90.

    (d) Joint Bn.H.Q. dugout at J.9.a.40.90.

    (e) New Bn. H.Q. dugout at J.3.c.25.35., 25% complete.

    (f) 24 Dugout Entrances Gas Proofed at E.28.d.60.70. E.28.d.98.90., J.9.a.35.95., E.28.a.05.02., SAILLY-AU-BOIS, and GOMMECOURT PARK KEEPS.

4. MISCELLANEOUS.

    (a) ROADS

        Shell Holes filled in and Roads repaired in Divisional Forward Area.

    (b) TRAMWAYS

        Trench Tramways patrolled, maintained, and repaired.

    (c) WATER SUPPLY

        Reserve Water Supply Tank erected in Battle Position on platform, sandbagged, and fitted with gas proof cover.

                                  forward.

(Cont'd.)   4.

(d) <u>BRIDGES</u>
  Bridge constructed at E.28.c.95.85. to carry limbers across Mule Track over AllSOPPS C.T.

  Footbridge constructed at E.28.c.90.85. over AllSOPPS C.T.

<u>RESUMÉ</u>

<u>WIRING</u> (NEW) Completed.   2,110 yds.

<u>TRENCHES</u>
  (a) (NEW) Completed   1,940 yds.
  (b) (OLD) Reconstructed 2,220 yds. 4,160 yds.

<u>DUGOUTS</u>
  (a) (DEEP)   completed 1
  (b) (ELEPHANT) 75%   "   20   2
                                       21
                          TOTAL   23.

13.6.18.   MAJOR.
        Cmdg. 2/5 Bn. loyal North lancs Rgt.(P)

DIARY.

2/5 BN. LOYAL NORTH LANCS REGT. (P).
SUPPLEMENTARY SUMMARY OF WORK COMPLETED DURING THE PERIOD OF
JUNE 12th. TO JUNE 29th. 1918.

1. **WIRING**

    (a) **RUM TRENCH**
    Erected 240 yards Single Apron Fence from K.9.b.80.70. to K.9.b.95.75.

    (b) **COMMECOURT TRENCH**
    Erected 220 yards Double Apron Fence from E.29.d.50.85. to E.29.d.30.80. and 360 yards Double Apron Fence from K.5.a.75.80. to E.29.c.78.20.

2. **TRENCHES**

    (a) **GUINNESS C.T. (Old Portion)**
    Widened and deepened 200 yards from K.4.c.70.70. to K.4.c.99.45.

    (b) **RAIL TRENCH (New Trench)**
    Excavated 540 yards of trench to Corps Pattern from E.29.d.80.10. to K.6.a.33.30. with fire steps made facing both flanks. Trench drained and 2 Sump pits excavated.

    (c) **TRAM TRENCH**
    Cleared 450 yards of trench from E.29.d.80.10. to K.5.a.70.83.

3. **DUGOUTS**

    (a) **FORT DICK** Two deep dugouts completed for M.G. H.Qs. at K.2.d.2.2.

forward./

(Cont'd.)

   (b) BEER TRENCH SYSTEM.

Two Infantry deep dugouts in B.0. and B.1. posts K.3.c.35.30. and K.3.c.60.50. each completed to 40%.

   (c) COIGNEUX

New Battn.H.Q. dugout at J.3.c.25.35. completed to 35%.

   (d) BEER TRENCH SYSTEM

Constructed 50 small elephant shelters in platoon and section posts as follows -

Post	Shelters	Post	Shelters
B.2. Post	5 Shelters.	B.3. Post	4 Shelters
B.4. "	3 "	B.6. "	5 "
B.b.1. "	4 "	B.b.2. "	4 "
B.b.3. "	4 "	B.b.4. "	4 "
B.b.5. "	4 "	B.b.6. "	4 "
B.c.1. "	2 "	B.c.2. "	3 "
B.c.3. "	2 "	B.c.4. "	2 "

   (e) RUM TRENCH

Constructed 2 small elephant shelters at K.3.d.99.05., 2 at K.4.c.05.10., 2 at K.4.d.25.25. and 4 at K.4.d.25.40.

   (f) COMMECOURT TRENCH

Constructed 3 small elephant shelters at E.29.d.25.90.

4. WATER POINTS

Water Points repaired as directed by O.C. 421 Field Coy. R.E.

5. TRANSPORT.

54 tons R.E. material transported to site of work - BEER TRENCH SYSTEM.

forward ./

RESUMÉ

WIRING (New) completed   820 yds.

TRENCHES
    (a) (New) completed.   540 yds.
    (b) (Old) Reconstructed.   650 yds.
                                           1190 yds

DUGOUTS
    (a) Deep. Completed.   2
        " 40% "   2
        " 35% "   1

    (b) Small Elephant.
            Completed.   55
                Total   60

                      Lieut' Colonel.
29.6.18.   Cmdg. 2/5 Bn. Loyal North Lancs Rgt. (P)

RESUMÉ

WORK COMPLETED DURING THE PERIOD MAY 7th/8th. to JUNE 29th/-1918

WIRING (New) Complete — 2930 yards

TRENCH
    (a) (New) complete — 2480 yds.
    (b) (Old) Reconstructed — 2870 "   5350 yards.

DUGOUTS
    (b) (Deep) Completed — 2
         " 40% " — 2
         " 35% " — 1
    (a) Small Elephant — 75

           Total — 80

29.6.18.
           Lieut. Colonel.
           Cmdg. 2/5 Bn. Loyal North Lancs Rgt.(P)

Weekly Report on Defence Works for week ending 6/6/18

Nature of Work	Location	No of Men	Coy	Unit	Factor of Completion	Remarks
1. WIRE	R.M.1 TRENCH. K.04.6.80. 26.10.4.60.0. GONNECOURT 77.3. K.5A.0H.40. T.26.5A.70.00.	24	A	—	45%	1'0-0 double c...ence added to existing wire.
2. TRENCHES AND STRONG POINTS.	K.20.30.35 TO K.4A.15.05 E.20A.40.90. TO E.20A.60.00.15	26	B	Do.	80%	APPROX 200 YDS wire entanglements added to existing wire
TRENCHES	E.20A.90.15 TO E.20A.05.15	16	B	Do.	94%	RUM TRENCH — repaired, deepened 94%. 5 sets of steps made.
	K.4A.90.45 TO K.4A.65.70	11	A	Do.	90%	GONNECOURT TR. cleaning & revetting where damaged. green camps
	E.2B.90.80. TO E.2B.30.B	23	F+G	Do.	35%	New excavation. GUINNESS CT cleaned & repaired (wet bottom of trench).
SECTION POSTS	K.5A.0.03. -5.	17	B	Do.	100%	ALLSOPPS CT cleaned & checkboarded. Revs added to Coys position.
	E.20A.70 N E.20A -5. 25.	8	B	Do.	100%	GONNECOURT TR 2 section posts complete
3. DUGOUTS.	K. 4A. 90. 10.	10	A	Do.	100%	Do Do Do Do
	E.4A.55.55.9. E.2A.70.10.	23	B	Do.	100%	4 Shelters complete (RUM TRENCH), one tunnelled openings
SMALL ELEPHANT SHELTERS.	E.5C. 6.90.9. E.4A.90.25	16	B	Do.	95%	2 Shelters Do
	E.29d. 56.00.	12	B	Do.	15%	2 Shelters Do
	K. 4d. 25. 25.	0	A	Do.	10%	4 Shelters Do
	K.1. A. 2. 4.	23	C	Do.	100%	2 Shelters Do
	K.2 D.2.2.	20	C	Do.	60%	Bde. H.Q. (Coy) under 502 Field Coy R.E. Excavating, timbering new frames & girders
	J 9a. 40.90	5	—	Do.	100%	Joint Battn Hq 20'x6' completed
	13Ca. 25.25.	10	H.Q.	Do.	—	New Batten Hq. disposed
4. DUGOUTS FITTED WITH ANTI-GAS BLANKETS	J. 9a. 40. 90.	5	—	—	—	One Entrance
5. M.G. POSITIONS.				NIL		
6. GENERAL. ROADS.	FORWARD AREA	7	A.	Do.		Shell holes filled in where necessary.
TRAMWAYS	Do.	6	A.	Do.		Tramways Repaired, where & where necessary.
BRIDGE.	E.2B. 60.20.	11	B.	Do.	100%	Bridge to carry mule track over ALLSOPPS C.T.
SUBTERRANEAN PASSAGE.	HR ROSSIGNOL FARM.	8	GROUPS	Do.		ASSISTING. 502 F.D COY. R.E.

6.6.18

MAJOR.
O.C. WORKS
2/5 LOYAL N LANCS REGT (P.)

WEEKLY REPORT ON DEFENCE WORKS for WEEK ENDING 23.6.9. REF SHEET 57D 1/10000
3/5 LOYAL N LANCS REGT (?)

NATURE OF WORK.	LOCATION	MAP REF.	BLOCK.	UNIT.	% OF COMPLETION	REMARKS
WIRING.	R.W TR. R.S/300.06.19	28	A		50%	Broken? down in places
	KARNAK TR. M20.16	28	A			m/g 1
	DORRIE COURT TR.					
TRENCHES & R.O.W. DUGOUTS	E.500.16.10. & E.400.16.10		A		60%	
	R.W 200 TR. O6.20.16.			A		
TRENCHES.	COUNTESS C.T. R.50.20.10 N	23	A	Do.	85%	
	OUT TR. N.T.20.20.10			Do.	90%	
	ANT. TR. A20.10.6.11.			Do.		
A. REDOUBTS.	R.500.06.01 K.4.6.10.11.12.	24	A	Do.		
B. "	SAME AS ABOVE	16	A	Do.	10%	
	" Do "	14	A	Do.		
ANTI-TANK ELECTRIC FLOOR	R.200.06.10.	6		Do.	50%	3
	E.700 TR. & E.S1.Ro.1	26	A	Do.	50%	2
	E.100 06.00. Do.	23	A	Do.	15%	
	E.500.06.10 & E.1.0.S.N	23	C		25%	M9
SHELTERED TROOPS.	K.N. & R.N.	15				
M.M.G's. FITTED WITH	J. 05.19.					
ANT. AND PLANKETS.	RO.100/4			NIL		
#1.2. POSITIONS						
5. GENERAL	JOHN REDWARD AREA	7	A	Do.		
	TRENCH TR. Do. Do.	7	B	Do.		
H.E.S. TANK.	K.Z.A. 0p.19	4	C	Do.	Complete	

Weekly Rpt on Defence Works for week ending 20.6.18. Ref Sheet 51 DNE
1/20,000

Nature of Work	Location	Men	Coy	Unit Tracts		
1) Wiring	Camn Ln. K.9b.80.70 To. K.9b.95.45.	24	A	2/5.	60%	240yds S.A. fence. 40yds D.A. fence
	Gommecourt Ln. E.29d.50.80.70.E.29d.50.80.	25	B	"	40%	220yds D.A. fence erected
	K.5a.80.85. 6 E.29c.78.20.	21	B.	"	40%	360yds Do
2) Trenches & Shrap Points	Guinness C.T.	10	A.	"	90%	Widening, deepening & repairing duckboards
	K.11c.9.70.70 K.4e.99.HS. New CT. (Rail Tunnel) E.29d.80.10 70 K.6a.33.30	449.	A. 18 & C.	"	100%	New tunnel. 50yds dug complete. (fire stepped on alternate sides
	Siam Tunnel. E.29d.80.10.	"	"	"	100%	Tunnel cleared complete.
3) Dugouts	To K.5a.40.83.					
	K-4c.05.10..x	13.	A	"	60%	2 Shelters
	K. 30d.99..05.. x	9.	A.	"	90%	2. Do.
	K. 4d.25..25.	12.	A.	"	28%	2 Do.
	E. 29d.15. 90.	26.	B	"	90%	3 Do
	K. 2d. 2. 2.	35.	C	"	90%	M.G. H.Q. dugouts
	K. 30. 35. 30 & K.3c.60.50	64	C.	"	7%	Inf. Dugouts (2 dugouts)
	J. 30. 25. 25	55	HQ.	"	30%	Bn. HQ. dugout.
4. Dugouts fitted with anti gas blankets.						
5. M.G. Postns.					Nil.	
6 General	Roads Forward Area	1.	A	"		Roads Tarentees & Fraines
	Tramways Do. Do	1.	A.	"		Tramways Do Do
	Water points	26.	HQ.	"		Work under 421 Field Coy R.E.
	P.A Shelters	26.	"	"		Do Do

P.A. Fahsttee (signature)

2/5 Loyal N. Lancs. Regt. (P)   Weekly Report on Defence Works for Week ending 27.6.18 (6.0 A.M.)   Ref. Sheet. 57 D N.E. 1/20,000

Nature of Work	Location	No. of Men.	Coy.	Unit.	Factor of Completion	Remarks
(1). Wiring.	Goodman Cs				NIL	
(2) Trenches or flying posts.	K.4.c.70.70 to K.4.c.99.45 Gunness .0.J.	30.	A.	2/5 L.N.L.R.	95%	150 yds. trench yet to be cleared.
(3) Dugouts.	K.3d. 99.06.	20.	A	Do	100%	2 Shelters
	K.4c. 05.10.	10	A	Do	100%	2 Do
	K.4d. 25.25.	10.	A	Do	100%	2 Do
	E.29d. 15.90.	30.	B.	Do	100%	3 Do
	Elephant Shelters in Posts – Beer Trench.					
SMALL ELEPHANT SHELTERS	System:- E.24c. E.24D. E.28a. K.3.A. K.3.B. K.30.	179.	A+C.	Do	Whole task 50 Shelters 74.6%	
	Total Shelters to be Constructed – 50	121	B.	Do		
Do. Do. Do.	K.4.D. 25. 40. K.2.D. 2.2. K.3.c. 35.30 & K.3c. 60.50 J.3e. 26. 35.	20 34. 64 13.	A. C. C.	Do. Do. Do. Do.	35% 40% 35%	M.G. H.Q. 2 Dugouts – One Complete. Infantry Dugouts 13.0 & B.1. Posts (40% complete. 12 men. 27 inst.) Battn H.Q. dugout.
Dugouts fitted with Anti-gas Blankets.					NIL	
M.G. Positions.					NIL	
General Roads	Toward Orea	17.	A.	Do.		Roads Labelled & Banned.
Tramways.	Do		A.	Do		Do Do
Water Points	Do	20	2nd	Do		Work under H.21 Field Coy. R.E.
R.A Shelters		26.		Do		Do Do

	B.2.		B.3		B.b.1.		B.b.2.		B.b.3		B.C.1		B.C.2
	No.1.	100%	No.1.	100%	No.1.	100%	No.1.	60%	No.1.	100%	No.1.	100%	No.1.	100%
	No.2.	100%	No.2.	65%	No.2.	100%	No.2.	100%	No.2.	100%	No.2.	100%	No.2.	100%
	No.3.	100%	No.3.	65%	No.3.	100%	No.3.	50%	No.3.	75%			No.3.	100%
	No.4.	100%	No.4.	40%	No.4.	50%	No.4.	100%	No.4.	65%				
	No.5.	100%	N											

C.0Y.

	B.4.		B.0		B.b.4		B.b.5.		B.b.6.		B.C.3		B.C.4
	No.1.	100%	No.1.	100%	No.1.	100%	No.1.	100%	No.1.	100%	No.1.	NIL	No.1.	NIL
	No.2.	100%	No.2.	100%	No.2.	100%	No.2.	100%	No.2.	100%	No.2.	NIL	No.2.	NIL
	No.3.	40%	No.3.	100%	No.3.	40%	No.3.	40%	No.3.	40%				
			No.4.	100%	No.4.	NIL	No.4.	NIL	No.4.	NIL				
			No.5.	100%										

H. Shelters (Rum Trench)

24.6.18

Cmmdg. 2/5 Loyal N. Lancs Regt.

Major 2/5 Loyal N. Lancs Regt.

Army Form C. 2118.

WAR DIARY
or
INTELLIGENCE SUMMARY.
(Erase heading not required)

Reg. No. ...A/172...
ORDERLY ROOM
DATE 1915
2/5 LOYAL NORTH LANCS

JULY 18.

Place	Date	Hour	Summary of Events and Information	Remarks and references to Appendices
COIGNEUX.	1st -2nd		Strength of Battalion:- 39 officers, 758. O.R's. Battalion was relieved by the New Zealand (Maori) Pioneer Battalion. as follows:- July 1st:- Headquarters moved to camp east of ST. LEGER-LES-AUTHIE. "1/2nd:- {"B" Company in GOMMECOURT WOOD who relieved. {2 platoons of "C" Coy. at BAYENCOURT were relieved. "2/3rd:- {"A" Company in GOMMECOURT WOOD who relieved. {2 platoons of "C" Coy. in GOMMECOURT PARK were relieved.	
ST.LEGER- -LES-AUTHIE	3rd 4th 5th 6th		Interior economy. Battalion employed in constructing huts & improving camp. "A" & "B" companies commenced training. "C" Company commenced work on the purple line, constructing deep dug-outs (in the rear) and baby elephant shelters in the vicinity of SAILLY AU BOIS, COURCELLES, BERTRAN COURT and BEAUSART.	

Army Form C. 2118.

WAR DIARY
of
INTELLIGENCE SUMMARY.
(Erase heading not required)

Instructions regarding War Diaries and Intelligence Summaries are contained in F. S. Regs., Part II. and the Staff Manual respectively. Title pages will be prepared in manuscript.

Place	Date	Hour	Summary of Events and Information	Remarks and references to Appendices
ST. LEGER-	7th		As on 6th inst.	
	8th - 12th		" " "	
	12th		"B" Coy. took out work from "C" Coy. who commenced training.	
	13th		"A" Company - training	
			"B" - Working parties.	
			"C" - training.	
	14th -19th		As on 13th inst.	
	20th		"A" Coy. took out work from "B" Coy. who commenced training.	
	21st		57th Div. Horse Show v Sports.	
	22nd		- do -	
LES-AUTHIE-	23rd		As per 20th inst.	
	24th		Battalion Sports.	

Army Form C. 2118.

WAR DIARY
or
INTELLIGENCE SUMMARY.
(Erase heading not required.)

Place	Date	Hour	Summary of Events and Information	Remarks and references to Appendices
ST.LEGER- -LES-AUTHIE -&-	25th- 28th Sept.		Work and training as on 23rd inst.	
	29th		The Division was transferred to G.H.Q. reserve in VI Corps. The Batt. admn moved to GROUCHES MILLY by road as part of the 19th Inf. Bde. Group.	
GROUCHES	30th		The Batt. also moved by road to WANQUETIN as part of the 19th Inf. Bde. Group.	
"	31st		Interior economy.	
			Strength of Battalion :- 42 Officers, 813 O.R.	

Confidential 16   9/19/19   R/5

WAR DIARY

OF

2/5 Bn. LOYAL NORTH LANCS.

From August 1st 1918.   To Aug 31st 1918.

Army Form C. 2118.

19.

WAR DIARY
or
INTELLIGENCE SUMMARY.

AUGUST.

Place	Date	Hour	Summary of Events and Information	Remarks and references to Appendices
WANQUETIN	1st		Battalion moved to billets in ARRAS. Transport lines at ANZIN.	
ARRAS	2nd–5th		Training and taking economy. Reconnoitring routes.	
"	6th		B and C coys moved to Bois de la Maison Blanche — nr BLANGY. HQ, A company and Q.M. Stores remained at ARRAS. Transport lines at ANZIN.	
"	7th		Coys commenced work on forward system:— A Cy. working under 190th Infy. Bde. B " " " 191st " " C " " " 192nd " "	
"	8th–11th		Work as for 7th inst.	
"	12th–18th		" " " " " "	

Army Form C. 2118.

WAR DIARY
or
INTELLIGENCE SUMMARY.
(Erase heading not required.)

August 19

Place	Date	Hour	Summary of Events and Information	Remarks and references to Appendices
ARRAS	18th		Battalion moved to MARQUAY as follows, and came into G.H.Q. reserve:—	
		7a.m.	1. Transport moved to MARQUAY.	
		1 p.m.	2. A & B. Coys " " "	
		"	3. H.Q's " " "	
		"	4. C & D Coys remained at ARRAS under orders of 140th Inft. Bde.	
			(N.B. Battalion was relieved by 61st Division.)	
MARQUAY	19th		Interior economy and training.	
"	20th		Training.	
"	21/22/23/24		Battalion moved to NOYELLE-VION and bivouaced in marsh north of BEAUDRICOURT and billetted.	
NOYELLE-VION	22/23/24 mid		— — —	
BEAUDRICOURT	25	3.35 p.m.	The Battalion moved to BAVINCOURT (in huts)	
BAVINCOURT	26/27 mid		The Battalion moved to BLAIREVILLE (in bivouac)	
BLAIREVILLE	27th	8.30 p.m.	The Battalion moved to bivouac at N.31.c.1.1. [Sheet 51b approx.] Relieved the	
"	30th	5 a.m.	The Battalion moved to bivouac at N.36.a.9.6. [Sheet 51b ed. 9000] M²A Notts &c Derbys. Going over went in hand	

WAR DIARY
or
INTELLIGENCE SUMMARY

Army Form C. 2118.

Place	Date	Hour	Summary of Events and Information	Remarks and references to Appendices
Sheet 51b & 10000				
N 25 a 9.1	30th	8am	Bm. the Battalion took over work of repairing all roads in forward area from HENINEL to CROISILLES	
	31st	8am	Strength of Bn. 24 officers, 70 rank	

19

Clifford

CONFIDENTIAL

WAR DIARY.

OF.

9/5 Bn. LOYAL NORTH LANCS.

From Sept 1st 1918
To Sept 30th 1918

Vol 20 5/5

Army Form C. 2118.

WAR DIARY
or
INTELLIGENCE SUMMARY.
(Erase heading not required)

SEPTEMBER (20)

Place	Date	Hour	Summary of Events and Information	Remarks and references to Appendices
Sunk E56.4.00m N.35.a.9.6.1st	Sept 1st	10 noon	Strength S/Battalion 34 Officers 70 ranks	
"	2nd		Battalion moved to U.15.c.8.6. (near CROISILLES) and was employed making sleeping dugouts, during the advance. Work as on 31st inst.	
"	3rd	2.30 pm		
O.50.c.8.6.	4th — 7th	6 pm 7 pm	"E" Coy moved to V.19.c. (near RIENCOURT). Battalion (less C Coy) moved to D.7.c.5.5. (QUEANT) & occupied dug-outs in the Hindenburg Line	
H.15.c.8.6.			Battalion employed in repairing & entering a sand between QUEANT and RIENCOURT. During the above period the Battalion kept in close touch with the advancing troops & were employed repairing & opening up communication & repairing old tracks.	
QUEANT	7th — 12th			

WAR DIARY
or
INTELLIGENCE SUMMARY

Army Form C. 2118.

September 20

Place	Date	Hour	Summary of Events and Information	Remarks and references to Appendices
QUEANT	13th–15th		Repairing roads in vicinity of QUEANT.	
"	16th		Battalion was relieved by 14th N.F. (60th Division) and moved by road to bivouac near ST LEGER (B4 b 2.1).	
ST. LEGER	17th–18th		Preparing camp, baths, kitchens &c. "C" Coy commenced work on roads at ECOUST. "A" " commenced training. "B" " baths.	
"	19th		B & C Coys working on roads at ECOUST. A Company training.	
"	20th–26th		Battalion who employed filling in shell craters in roads & repairing roads in the vicinity of St Leger and Ecoust.	
"	26th		Companies moved forward for operations and were attached as follows:— A Coy. to 51st Bn M.G.C. B Coy. to 421 Fd. Coy RE	

WAR DIARY
or
INTELLIGENCE SUMMARY.
(Erase heading not required.)

Army Form C. 2118.

September 20

Place	Date	Hour	Summary of Events and Information	Remarks and references to Appendices
ST LEGER	27th (cont)		C Coy 16 505 Fd. Coy. R.E.	
			B.H.Q., Transport, Q.M. Stores and surplus personnel remained at St Leger.	
	28th		Buttes moved to PRONVILLE	
	29th		do to E.22.c.3.6. (Sheet 57cNE 20,000) 2 miles East of MOEUVRES	
ENCIS.b.	30th	noon	and the work of Coy. travel was supervised. Strength of Bn. Officers	

21/

CONFIDENTIAL

WAR DIARY. Vol 21 P/57

OF

2/5 LOYAL NORTH LANCS.

From October 1st 1918.

To Oct. 31. 1918.

WAR DIARY
INTELLIGENCE SUMMARY.

Army Form C. 2118.

OCTOBER

Place	Date	Hour	Summary of Events and Information	Remarks and references to Appendices
57.CENT. E.99 c.2.6.	1st	12 noon	Strength of Battalion 39 officers 960 other ranks. Battalion HQ moved from trenches west of BOURLON WOOD to bivouacs in a sunken road S.W. of FONTAINE - NOTRE - DAME. Distribution of companies as follows :— A Coy :— Attached to 157th Am. M.G.C. for carrying. B " " " 421 Fld. Coy. R.E. repairing roads. C " " " 506 " " " "	
FONTAINE NOTRE DAME	2nd 3rd		Work as above.	
"	4th		Companies rejoined the Battalion. It continued repairing roads in the forward area together with the construction of trenches & strong points in the MARCOING line.	
"	5th-9th		Work as above.	
"	10th		Battalion moved by road from FONTAINE NOTRE DAME to bivouacs at MOEUVRES.	

WAR DIARY
or
INTELLIGENCE SUMMARY.

Army Form C. 2118.

Place	Date	Hour	Summary of Events and Information	Remarks and references to Appendices
MOEUVRES	11th		Interior economy.	
	12th	13.30.	Battalion marched to HERMES and entrained — detained at FOUQEREUIL, and marched to billets at NOEUX-LE-MINES.	
NOEUX-LES-MINES.	13th		Battalion arrived 5 a.m. Rested during the rest of the day.	
	14th		Battalion marched to VAVDRI COURT, and travelled by bus to PONT LOGY (ESTAIRES - LA BASSEE road). Marched to bivouacs at FROMELLES.	
FROMELLES.	15th		A C Coy. moved slightly forward in accordance with orders allotted, that alive during relieved the 9th R.W.F.(?) - 17th Div?.	
	16th		B, H.Q's moved to trenches near RADINGHEM and coy. areas also went forward to trenches in vicinity of RADINGHEM.	
RADINGHEM.	17th		Work in Whitcom forward area.	
	18th		Battalion supron by man to billets in CANTELEU.	
CANTELEU	19th		The Battalion provided a guard of honour to M. CLEMENCEAU.	

WAR DIARY
or
INTELLIGENCE SUMMARY.

Army Form C. 2118.

21

Place	Date	Hour	Summary of Events and Information	Remarks and references to Appendices
CANTELEU	20th		Memorable the occasion of his visit to the city of LILLE after four years captivity. That signing took place amongst the civilian population a large majority of the 700,000 left behind taking part in the demonstration making one of the outstanding events in the history of the French Republic. Bn moved by road to LEZENNES. Distribution of companies as follows:— A — HELLEMMES. B — RONCHIN. C — HELLEMMES.	
LEZENNES	21st		Battalion concentrated at LEZENNES. Moved by road to CORNET.	
"	22nd		Battalion employed in roads in forward area in vicinity of BLANDAIN and FROYENNES.	
"	23rd-27th		As in 22nd.	

Army Form C. 2118.

WAR DIARY
or
INTELLIGENCE SUMMARY.
(Erase heading not required.)

21.

Place	Date	Hour	Summary of Events and Information	Remarks and references to Appendices
CORNET.	28th		Work as on the 29th inst.	
"	29th		" "	
"	30th		" "	
"	31st		Battalion was relieved by the 4th Royal Welsh Fus. (47th Div.) & marched route to RONCHIN. (BILLETED)	
			Strength of Battalion. 38 Officers. 742 O.R.	

WAR DIARY.
NOVEMBER Vol 22

2/5 L. N. LANCS

WAR DIARY
INTELLIGENCE SUMMARY

Army Form C. 2118.

NOVEMBER (22)

Place	Date	Hour	Summary of Events and Information	Remarks and references to Appendices
RONCHIN	1st } 2nd - } 9th }		Strength of Battalion :- 39 Officers. 750 O.R. Battalion carried on with training. One party was detailed to supervise work done by Portuguese at MARQUAIN.	
RONCHIN	10th		Bn. moved by march route to BLANDAIN.	
BLANDAIN	11th		Bn. moved by march route to TOURNAI and was billeted in RUE DE L'ATHENEE.	
TOURNAI	12th } 20th }		The Battalion was employed on railway construction. The metals east of TOURNAI were opened & work was also done on TOURNAI Station.	
TOURNAI	21st } 22nd } 30th }		Battalion moved by march route to billets in RONCHIN. Battalion did training daily. In addition, educational subjects were introduced and classes were carried on daily. Recreation was also indulged in as much as possible.	

WAR DIARY "S.A.D.O.S S-Y.P.S." Army Form C. 2118.

or

INTELLIGENCE SUMMARY.

NOVEMBER 1918

(Erase heading not required.)

Hour, Date, Place	Summary of Events and Information	Remarks and references to Appendices
Petit Porichon	Daily Routine and tour of Units	
1st		
2nd "	Do	
3rd "	Do	
4th "	Do	6 tons stores rec'd from Base
5th "	Do	6 tons Rugs Horse & Gd Cooks rec'd from Case
6th "	Do	
7th "	Do	10 tons rec'd from Base
8th "	Do	
9th "	Do	13 tons stores & vehicles received from Base
10th "	Do	
11th "	Do	11 tons stores & Clothing — Do —
12th "	Do	
13th "	Do	11 tons stores — Do —
14th "	Do	12 Cookers and 2 Vehicles — Do —
15th "	Do	
16th "	Do	6 tons stores & 3 Vehicles rec'd from Base
17th "	Do	
18th "	Do	16 tons stores and 1,000 Blankets (2nd hindrance) rec'd from Base.
19th "	Do	2 vehicles received from Base
20th "	Do	
21st "	Do	10 tons stores received from Base. 2nd winter Blanket issue Completed
22nd "	Do	2 Vehicles received from Case
23rd "	Do	5 tons general stores received from Base
24th "	Do	
25th "	Do	wired Parts to stop move pending move of Division
26th "	Do	
27th "	Do	
28th "	Do	
29th "	Do	
30th "	Do	

M.Moore
Major
S.A.D.O.S. S.Y.P.S.

WAR DIARY
2/5 K.L.R. (D)

Army Form C. 2118.

DECEMBER (23)

WAR DIARY
or
INTELLIGENCE SUMMARY.
(Erase heading not required.)

Place	Date	Hour	Summary of Events and Information	Remarks and references to Appendices
RONCHIN	1st		Strength of Battalion 35 Officers 960 O.Rs.	
RONCHIN	2nd		Bn. marched to CAMPHIN au gres of the 141 Bde.	
CAMPHIN	3rd		Bde Sports.	
ARRAS	4th		Bn marched to ARRAS as past of the 71st Bde Group.	
			Bn. billeted in the MUSEUM, ARRAS with HdQrs in Rue au Doigt Visagi.	
ARRAS	5th - 23rd		Bn. Coys. attached to Bde. Artillery, finding knee improving accommodation, & evening an week standing. Regt. orders preparing for 51st Div. work in ARRAS Reserve, preparing from 51st Div. Camphin home.	
ARRAS	24th 25th 26th		Xmas Celebrations.	
ARRAS	27th - 31st		Battalion worked in reserve as above.	
			Strength of Bn. 34 Off. 660 O.Rs.	

2/5 Bn
Loyal North Lancs
Regt

WAR DIARY
JANUARY 1919

WAR DIARY or INTELLIGENCE SUMMARY

JANUARY 24

Place	Date	Hour	Summary of Events and Information	Remarks and references to Appendices
ARRAS	1st		Strength of Battalion:- 36 officers. 660 O.Rs. Battalion commenced training in preparation for G.O.C's inspection.	
ARRAS	2nd–4th		Training &c. as in the 1st	
	5th		Two platoons were attached to 54th M.G. Artillery making horse standings. Remainder of Battalion carried on training for inspection.	
–do–	6th–9th		Training.	
–do–	10th		The Battalion was inspected by G.O.C. 54th Division on the Grande Place, Arras.	
–do–	11th		15 cpls were attached to 54th M.G. Artillery, making accommodation (horse standings).	
–do–	12th–16th		Work for Divl. Artillery, salvage & improving billets.	J.M.

WAR DIARY
or
INTELLIGENCE SUMMARY.

Army Form C. 2118.

January

(24)

Place	Date	Hour	Summary of Events and Information	Remarks and references to Appendices
ARRAS	17 31		Work on our 18" Strength of Bn. 32 Officers 476 O.Rs.	M.

P/57

FEB. 1919

WAR DIARY P/57

2/5 K.O.Y.L.I.

WAR DIARY or INTELLIGENCE SUMMARY

Army Form C. 2118.

FEBRUARY

Place	Date	Hour	Summary of Events and Information	Remarks and references to Appendices
MARK	Feb 1-28		Strength of Battalion. 32 Officers 476 O.R. During the month the B[attalio]n were employed in Salvage work in the town of Arras and the surrounding districts. Burhps were formed and ammunition leave in training for removal to assist in work at the transit duties of Arras were found by the unit. Demobilisation went on very rapidly, the following list giving the numbers of men demobilised during the month:— Feb 1st 12 Feb 11th 6 Feb 26 23 " 2nd 16 " 13th 2 " 27 39 " 3rd 3 " 14th 3 " 6th 7 " 15th 5 " 7th 3 " 16th 13 " 8th 17 " 19th 70 TOTAL 219	

Place	Date	Hour	Summary of Events and Information	Remarks and references to Appendices
AARE	3rd		Church Parade 24 April 227. OR	

War Diary Vol 26
March 1911
2/5 Loyal North Lancs. Regt

WAR DIARY
or
INTELLIGENCE SUMMARY

Army Form C. 2118

March

Place	Date	Hour	Summary of Events and Information	Remarks and references to Appendices
MAROEUIL	13th 24th 27th		To Army of Occupation — 3 offs. 27 ORs. For Demobilisation — 6 offs. 73 ORs.	
	31st		Strength of Battalion — 12 offs.	

WAR DIARY
or
INTELLIGENCE SUMMARY.
(Erase heading not required.)

Army Form C. 2118.

MARCH.

Place	Date	Hour	Summary of Events and Information	Remarks and references to Appendices
ARRAS	1st – 17th		Strength of Battalion 24 Officers 228 other ranks. During this period very little work could be undertaken owing to the influx and demobilisation's to drafts the dispatched to Army of Occupation.	
	18th		Battalion moved by road route to MAROEUIL, & reconcentrated in Hutments.	
MAROEUIL	19th to 31st		Intensive Economy & cleaning & overhauling of Mobilisation Stores carried out. Vehicles washed.	
			During the month the following drafts left the Battalion :—	
	6th		to Army of Occupation – 3 Offs. 50 ORs	
	10th		" " 2 " 54 ORs	
	28th		" " 20 ORs	

WAR DIARY

2/5 Royal North Lancs

April 1917

Army Form C. 2118

WAR DIARY
or
INTELLIGENCE SUMMARY
(Erase heading not required.)

APR 1919

Place	Date	Hour	Summary of Events and Information	Remarks and references to Appendices
MARDEON	1st		Strength of Battalion 12 Officers 43 other ranks.	
	1st to 30th		The Battalion rapidly reduced to Cadre Establishment. Overhauling & cleaning of Mobilisation Stores continued during month.	
	30th		Strength 6 Officers 56 other ranks.	

CONFIDENTIAL 9/8/28

WAR DIARY

OF

1/5 Royal North Lancs. Regt.

MAY 1919

Army Form C. 2118

WAR DIARY
or
INTELLIGENCE SUMMARY
(Erase heading not required.)

28 May 1919

Place	Date	Hour	Summary of Events and Information	Remarks and references to Appendices
MARŒUIL	1-31		Strength of Battalion 6 Officers 56 other ranks. Salvage collected & put into dump ready for removing.	
	2?		Reduction of Cadre establishment by 7.5%. 2 2 other ranks became available for demobilisation.	
	3/24		Strength of Battalion 4 Officers 51 other ranks.	

CC

www.ingramcontent.com/pod-product-compliance
Lightning Source LLC
Chambersburg PA
CBHW081449160426
43193CB00013B/2415